HEBREWS

HOW JESUS SPEAKS INTO EVERYTHING

Other studies in the Not Your Average Bible Study series

Ruth

Psalms

Jonah

Malachi

Sermon on the Mount

Ephesians

Colossians

James

1 Peter

2 Peter and Jude

1–3 John

For updates on this series, visit lexhampress.com/nyab

HEBREWS

HOW JESUS SPEAKS INTO EVERYTHING

NOT YOUR AVERAGE BIBLE STUDY

JOHN D. BARRY

LEXHAM PRESS

Hebrews: How Jesus Speaks Into Everything
Not Your Average Bible Study

Copyright 2014 Lexham Press
Adapted with permission from content originally published in *Bible Study Magazine* (Issues 1.1–2.3)

Lexham Press, 1313 Commercial St., Bellingham, WA 98225
LexhamPress.com

ISBN 978-1-57-799543-2

Academic Editor: Michael S. Heiser
Assistant Editors: Lynnea Fraser, Jessi Strong, Elizabeth Vince, Joel Wilcox
Cover Design: Christine Gerhart
Typesetting: ProjectLuz.com

CONTENTS

HOW TO USE THIS RESOURCE

Not Your Average Bible Study is a series of in-depth Bible studies that can be used for individual or group study. Depending on your individual needs or your group pace, you may opt to cover one lesson a week or more.

Each lesson prompts you to dig deep into the Word—as such, we recommend you use your preferred translation with this study. The author used his own translation, but included quotations from the English Standard Version. Whatever Bible version you use, please be sure you leave ample time to get into the Bible itself.

To assist you, we recommend using the Faithlife Study Bible, which is also edited by John D. Barry. You can download this digital resource for free for your tablet, phone, personal computer, or use it online. Go to FaithlifeBible.com to learn more.

May God bless you in the study of His Word.

INTRODUCTION

When we read the book of Hebrews, we encounter a community of Christians living in a time of trial—a community not so different from yours or mine. They, like us, were struggling to understand God in the midst of suffering. The message of the book is our message—their story is our story.

HEBREWS 1

Throughout the book of Hebrews, the author states that the community must learn to hold fast to their confession and all it entails. In this study, we will learn what type of confession the author had in mind and how it was to be personally and communally lived out. By learning what the book states in its own right and in its own context, we will learn what God is saying to us in our circumstances.

Deeply rooted in the sermon delivered to the Hebrews is a sense of urgency. The same sense of urgency exists today. We too suffer from spiritual depravity and lack of community. Our study of the book will help us understand the pressing needs of ancient believers and answer the cry of our own. By understanding how God equipped them, we will understand how He can outfit us. In this ancient text, we find modern answers.

OPEN THE BOOK— READ IT AND PRAY IT

Take a moment to pray that the Holy Spirit will illuminate this book.

Read the Book of Hebrews aloud in one setting (all 13 chapters).

In the Graeco-Roman and Jewish world, letters (like those in the New Testament) were read aloud in front of a group of people. Likewise, Hebrews, a sermon converted into a letter, would have been read aloud.

Reflect upon what stuck out to you as primary themes, ideas, or messages. How would these things affect a community living after Jesus' resurrection in a time of political, military, and social uprisings?

_____

_____

_____

_____

Imagine that your place of worship, your home, and your community is being destroyed simply because you look a certain way or practice a certain religion. How would this influence your interpretation of the book?

_____

_____

_____

_____

_____

OPEN THE BOOK— READ IT AND TAKE NOTES

Pray that God would reveal himself to you through this book.

Closely (and slowly) read the book of Hebrews again.

Write down your questions. Let the text speak for itself, and let God speak through it. This will allow you to discern God's will for your life.

_____

_____

_____

_____

_____

Make any links you can between the different parts of the book. Look at how the book has been paragraphed in your Bible and ask yourself which paragraphs correspond with other ones.

_____

_____

_____

_____

_____

Look for key grammatical markers like "therefore," "but," and "now." Underline or highlight them. These grammatical terms are a way of marking a shift in an author's thoughts.

THE CONNECTION BETWEEN LONG AGO AND TODAY

Pray that God would reveal His plan for humanity to you through this book.

Read Hebrews 1:1–4. Reflect on 1:1–2.

What has occurred "long ago"? Whom did God speak "to" and whom did He speak "by"? What does this tell us about how God spoke in the past?

_____

_____

_____

_____

What has occurred in "these last days"? Whom is God speaking "by" in "these last days"? What does this tell us about how God currently speaks?

_____

_____

_____

_____

Are we still living in "these last days"? What (if anything) has changed since the author wrote this book around AD 68? Why are these last days lasting so long?

_____

_____

_____

Is there an intentional switch between what has occurred "long ago" and what is occurring in "these last days"? What does this say about the significance of God's Son entering the world?

_____

_____

_____

_____

What is God's Son the heir of? What did God do through His Son?

_____

_____

_____

_____

Is there a link between God's Son and God's ability to create?

_____

_____

_____

_____

There is an allusion to Psalm 2:8 in this passage. What does the author's reflection on this psalm tell us about God's Son and God's plan for humanity? (Keep in mind that the author is interpreting a book written centuries before).

_____

_____

_____

_____

THE SON'S IDENTITY

Pray that God would reveal Himself to you through the power of His Word.

Read Hebrews 1:1–4. Reflect on 1:3–4.

What is the identity and role of the Son?

_____

_____

_____

What kind of imagery is the author evoking in this passage? Use a concordance to look up the use of the word "glory" in the Old Testament (specifically in Exodus and the Psalms).

_____

_____

_____

_____

What does being God's Son entail? What is the meaning of this term in the book of Hebrews, and in the rest of the Bible? Are any other individuals called "sons of God"? Look at Psalm 29:1 and 89:6 (the literal translation of "heavenly beings" is "sons of God" in these passages).

_____

_____

_____

In the first century, angels (sons of God) were believed to be God's warriors and messengers. Could this be the reason why the author states that the Son is superior to the angels?

_____

_____

_____

Is the Son's superiority a theme in other places in the book?

_____

_____

_____

_____

Why is it important that the Son is superior to the angels?

_____

_____

_____

Where does the author provide support for the claim that the Son is superior to the angels?

_____

_____

_____

SUPPORT FOR THE SON'S UNIQUE SUPERIORITY

Pray that God would reveal His Son's superiority over all your struggles.

Read Hebrews 1:1–4. Reflect on 1:5–6.

The author quotes Psalm 2:7 in Hebrews 1:5a—Read Psalm 2. What is the theme of this psalm? What figures are involved? How is God characterized? Why would the author choose to quote this passage?

_____

_____

_____

_____

_____

The author quotes 2 Samuel 7:14 in Hebrews 1:5b—Read 2 Samuel 7:1–17. What is the message of this story? What characters are involved? What is the significance of verse 14 in 2 Samuel 7:1–17? What theme does Psalm 2 and 2 Samuel 7:1–17 share in common?

_____

_____

_____

_____

_____

The author quotes Deuteronomy 32:43 from the Greek translation of the Old Testament (the Septuagint) in Hebrews 1:6a. The Septuagint reads "sons of God" here, but Hebrews reads "angels." What is the difference between the "sons of God" and the "Son of God"? (Think about lesson 4). What does this tell us about the role of the Son in the heavenly and earthly realm?

_____

_____

_____

_____

_____

_____

How does the Son's unique superiority affect our lives?

_____

_____

_____

_____

_____

THE ANOINTED SON

Pray that God would reveal His anointed Son to you.

Read Hebrews 1:1–4. Reflect on 1:7–12.

The author quotes Psalm 104:4 in 1:7—read Psalm 104. What does this passage tell us about angels?

_____

_____

_____

The author quotes Psalm 45:6–7 in Hebrews 1:8—read Psalm 45. In the Old Testament, this passage was about God, but the author states that it is about the Son. The author makes God and the Son one in the same. What does this tell us about the relationship of the Son and the Father? Who is anointed in Psalm 45? Who does the anointing in Psalm 45?

_____

_____

_____

_____

In Hebrews 1:10 the author quotes Psalm 102:25–27—Read Psalm 102. What are the primary themes of Psalm 102?

_____

_____

_____

How is the Lord characterized? What does Psalm 102 tell us about the roles of angels, the Son, and the Father?

_____

_____

_____

_____

_____

Why does the author of Hebrews choose passages that emphasize the power and eternality of the Father and the Son? (Think about the type of community being addressed).

_____

_____

_____

_____

_____

What is the message of this passage? How does the Son's anointed status affect the created order of the heavens and the earth?

_____

_____

_____

_____

_____

INHERITORS OF SALVATION

Pray that God would reveal the way you can inherit salvation.

Read Hebrews 1:1–14. Reflect on 1:13–14.

In Hebrews 1:13 the author quotes Psalm 110:1—Read Psalm 110. What does this passage indicate about the relationship between God the Father and the Son? Who is the psalm about (according to the psalm itself)? What themes emerge in Psalm 110 that have already surfaced in Hebrews 1?

_____

_____

_____

_____

Reflect on Psalm 110:4. What shift occurs between verse 4 and 5 in the psalm? How is this shift reflected in Hebrews? (Think specifically about the Son's kingship, unique relationship with God, His anointing, and His priesthood).

_____

_____

_____

_____

Who are the ministering spirits referred to in Hebrews 1:14?

_____

_____

_____

What are the ministering spirits sent out to do? For whose sake are the ministering spirits sent out? (Ponder what you have learned about the ministering spirits in the psalms that we have examined).

_____

_____

_____

_____

What is the difference between the ministering spirits and the Son?

_____

_____

_____

_____

How does one inherit salvation?

_____

_____

_____

_____

WHAT WE KNOW NOW

🤚 *Pray that God would engrave the message of Hebrews 1:1–14 on your heart.*

📄 *Reflect on Hebrews 1:1–14. Reflect upon what you have learned so far.*

Create a chart that shows the relationship between God the Father, the Son, and the ministering spirits.

What does Hebrews 1:1–4 tell us about the Son's identity in relation to God?

_____

_____

_____

_____

Reflect on 1:4. Based upon 1:5–14, how is the Son superior to the angels? How is the name He has inherited more excellent than theirs?

_____

_____

_____

What makes the Son unique?

_____

_____

_____

How does the Son's role as co-creator and preeminent, divinely appointed speaker on God's behalf influence our lives?

_____

_____

_____

What does the author of Hebrews want us to learn?

_____

_____

_____

Has the Son changed the course of history and brought perspective to suffering? In what ways has He made a seemingly distant God immanent (close to us)?

_____

_____

_____

CONCLUSION

We all too often lose sight of what we have witnessed and heard, or we simply believe we can no longer witness or hear anything. God has spoken and created through His Son. God continues to speak (in many forms) to people and create new life in them. God has made His exact imprint known in His Son. May you see this imprint reflected in your life and in the lives of others.

May you see, know, and feel the superiority of the Son in your life—His superiority over all the created order, heaven, and earth. And may you inherit the salvation that was witnessed to prior to His birth and continues to be spoken "in him in these last days."

May God speak new creation into your life. May His sacrifice heal your wounds and guide you through whatever circumstances you are enduring. May He bring you great joy in His creation, in His speech and in His Son.

HEBREWS 2

In our studies on Hebrews 1, we encountered a community of Christians living in a time of trial, a community not so different from yours or mine. They, like us, struggled to understand God in the midst of suffering. A sermon ("word of exhortation"; Heb 13:22), was delivered to this struggling group, a sermon which we now have in the book of Hebrews. We have much to learn from the ancient message of Hebrews. Like the group of people the author addressed, we too suffer from temptations and pain. The message of the book is our message—their story is our story.

WHAT WE HAVE HEARD— THE GREAT SALVATION

Pray that God would reveal how He has brought His great salvation.

Read Hebrews 1:1-2:18. Reflect on 2:1-3.

What are we to "pay much closer attention to," and why? What is the significance of this phrase? Does it provide a theme for the chapter?

_____

_____

_____

_____

Whose message "proved to be reliable"? In what verses are these messengers previously referenced and why?

_____

_____

_____

_____

What verse does the entire statement in 2:2 and the first statement in 2:3 provide support for?

_____

_____

_____

_____

The author uses the plural "we," referring to all of us in 2:3. In light of this, what does the author's rhetorical question about the "great salvation" indicate? Reflect on 1:1–14, and see who the bringer of the great salvation is.

_____

_____

_____

_____

_____

How was the "great salvation" declared, and by whom? When was it attested, and by whom? Note the similarities of 2:3 with 1:1.

_____

_____

_____

_____

_____

Does it feel like we have stopped paying "attention to what we have heard"? How can we pay better attention?

_____

_____

_____

_____

_____

HOW GOD REVEALS HIMSELF

Pray that the multiplicity of ways God reveals Himself would be made real to you.

Read Hebrews 2:1–18. Reflect on 2:1–5.

Hebrews 2:4 tells us of four things God has done to reveal Himself. What are these four things?

1. _____

2. _____

3. _____

4. _____

Hebrews 2:5 is a supporting point to 2:1, and the overall argument of 1:1. In light of this, what is the point of 2:1–5?

_____

_____

_____

_____

What is the impact of recognizing who the ultimate ruler of the world is?

_____

_____

_____

_____

In what ways can we allow the Word of God and the work of God's Son to penetrate more parts of our life?

_____

_____

_____

_____

_____

THE ONE CROWNED WITH GLORY AND HONOR

Pray that God would reveal to you His Son and the power of His reign.

Read Hebrews 2:1–18. Reflect on 2:6–8.

Hebrews 2:6b–8a is a quote from Psalm 8:4–6. Read Psalm 8. What is the primary theme of the psalm? What light does this psalm shed on the author's argument about the Son's place in the world, and among the heavenly beings?

_____

_____

_____

_____

The author uses "son of God" terminology in chapter 1. What is the author's intention in using a quote that refers to the "son of man" in this passage?

_____

_____

_____

_____

The author views Psalm 8:4–6 as prophetic. What does this prophecy emphasize about the Son?

_____

_____

_____

What is He "crowned" with? What is subjected to Him?

_____

_____

_____

_____

_____

The author draws a conclusion in 2:8b from Psalm 8:4–6. What is this conclusion?

_____

_____

_____

_____

_____

Does the Son's reign consist of power over your life? If so, what does this look like? Could you allow for Him to reign more?

_____

_____

_____

_____

_____

THE THINGS WE DO NOT SEE

Pray that God would reveal to you how He accomplished His purposes in His Son.

Read Hebrews 2:1–18. Reflect on 2:8–10.

Hebrews 2:8 states that we currently do not see "everything in subjection to him." (He rules over currently present things, and will rule in the future). What is the significance of the Son reigning over what we do not see?

_____

_____

_____

_____

The Son is named for the first time in the book of Hebrews in 2:9. What is the significance of this?

_____

_____

_____

_____

Why was the Son "made lower than the angels" "for a little while"? Who did the Son do this for?

_____

_____

_____

_____

Hebrews 2:10 makes a statement about why it was fitting for the Son to accomplish God's purposes. What is the author's reasoning here?

_____

_____

_____

_____

"For whom and by whom [do] all things exist"? (Read carefully, this is a bit tricky).

_____

_____

_____

_____

Through the scriptural quotations in Hebrews 1, the "sons" became a subject of interest in the book. What does Jesus accomplish for the "sons"? What is the Son the "founder of" and how does He "perfect" it?

_____

_____

_____

_____

How does the Son's ultimate control over heaven and earth impact our lives? Why should we allow for the Son to have control over our lives?

_____

_____

_____

_____

THE SOURCE OF SATISFACTION

Pray that God would reveal to you what it means for Him to call you "brother" or "sister."

Read Hebrews 2:1–18. Reflect on 2:11–13.

The first statement in 2:11 is support for an above point. What point is it supporting?

_____

_____

_____

What, or who, is the "source" of "he who sanctifies" and "those who are sanctified"? What are the implications of "he who sanctifies" and "those who are sanctified" having the same source?

_____

_____

_____

_____

Who is the "He" and the "them" in the phrase "That is why he is not ashamed to call them brothers"?

_____

_____

_____

The quotation in Hebrews 2:12 is from Psalm 22:22. The author attributes those words to Jesus. What does this tell us about the role of the Son prior to His coming to earth? Is Jesus a co-author of Psalm 22? Read and reflect upon Psalm 22. Who is the "congregation" in Psalm 22:22? (The idea of the angels is also present here, so think about who gathers around God in the heavens). A different verse from this psalm is quoted by Jesus—what verse is quoted and where? What are the implications of this psalm being so widely quoted by Jesus? What does it tell us about His character and divine role?

In Hebrews 2:13 there are quotations from Isaiah 8:17 and 18. Read and reflect upon Isaiah 8. What group of people is referenced in 8:16? What is the connection between this passage and Psalm 22:22? Who is doing the "trusting" and who is being "trusted in," in Isaiah 8:17 and in Hebrews 2:13? (They may not be the same people in both passages).

How can your actions toward God better show your appreciation for the tremendous things He has done for you in His Son?

THE DIVINE ONE WHO FREES US FROM SLAVERY

Pray that God would reveal to you why He sent His son.

Read Hebrews 2:1–18. Reflect on 2:14–15.

In the end of Hebrews 2:13 there is a quotation from Isaiah 8:18. By using this quote, the author refers to the people of God as the "children" of Jesus. What are the implications of us being both Jesus' brothers and sisters, as well as His children? (There are two different theological meanings at work here, both worth pondering.)

_____

_____

_____

_____

_____

Is it possible that the Son, when He becomes flesh, gets temporarily demoted to the level of His children (those born of the creation which was made through Him)? In what way does Hebrews 2:7 explain 2:14? What is the role of sanctification in all of this?

_____

_____

_____

_____

_____

Why did the Son become "flesh and blood?" What happened through the
Son's death?

_____

_____

_____

_____

Does Hebrews 2:14 indicate that the Son has destroyed the devil?

_____

_____

_____

How does "fear of death" enslave us? Is death itself a form of "slavery"? Could
both "slavery" and "death" be metaphors in this passage for something else?
(Read Rom 6.)

_____

_____

_____

_____

How can we be free from the things that enslave us? What has the Son brought
us that nobody else can?

_____

_____

_____

_____

A MERCIFUL AND FAITHFUL HIGH PRIEST

Pray that God would reveal to you how His Son paid for your sins.

Read Hebrews 2:1–18. Reflect on 2:16–17.

Hebrews 2:16 supports the first statement in 2:14. What does the statement in 2:16 tell us about the kind of thinking the author is opposing?

_____

_____

_____

_____

Who are the "offspring of Abraham" mentioned in 2:16? (See Psa 105:6; Isa 41:8; Jer 33:26; John 8:33–37; and 2 Cor 11:22).

_____

_____

_____

_____

Hebrews 2:17 begins with the word "therefore," which creates a connection back to previous statements. What statements is it summarizing?

_____

_____

_____

_____

What does it mean for the Son of God "to be made like his brothers in every respect"? What are the results of this?

_____

_____

_____

_____

Using Bible software, search for the phrase "high priest." What is the role of the high priest in Israel? Is the high priest usually merciful and faithful in the service of God?

_____

_____

_____

_____

Read Leviticus 23:26–32. Describe the purpose of the act the high priest performs in this passage. The word translated as "propitiation" has to do with this act. What does it mean for the "Son of God" to be "made lower than the angels," become "flesh and blood," and then perform this act?

_____

_____

_____

_____

What is the impact of the actions of the Son on your life?

_____

_____

_____

_____

THE ONE WHO CAN HELP US WHEN WE ARE TEMPTED

Pray that God would reveal to you the life-changing power of His Son.

Read Hebrews 2:1–18. Reflect on 2:18.

Hebrews 2:18 says that the Son suffered when tempted. Do suffering and temptation go hand-in-hand?

_____

_____

_____

_____

Who is attempting to reign over this world? (See 2:14).

_____

_____

_____

_____

Why is the Son able to help those who are being tempted?

_____

_____

_____

_____

How should we approach God when we are being tempted? Does the Son have power to intercede between us and God?

_____

_____

_____

_____

_____

What are the implications of the work of the Son upon all parts of your life?

_____

_____

_____

_____

_____

CONCLUSION

We feel distant from Jesus when we become convinced that we cannot relate to Him. The book of Hebrews teaches the opposite: The Son suffered when He was tempted, and because of this He is able to help us. The Son is victorious over the powers of heaven and the earth. The Son became our brother, even though we are meant to be His children. (Will you ever think of the phrase "brother (or sister) in Christ" the same again?) Although He for a time became lower than the angels, He has been crowned with glory because He was (and is) a faithful and merciful high priest. The Son made the sacrifice necessary for us to be one with God again—now and eternally.

May you realize that the Son can relate to your temptations and to your pain. May you seek the Son and find in Him new life and new hope.

HEBREWS 3-4

Every day presents new trials and challenges, but the words of Hebrews have the power to comfort and inspire us. We've learned that the author of Hebrews found hope in the life, death, and resurrection of the Son of God, and in turn delivered a sermon ("word of exhortation"; Heb 13:22) to a struggling community (10:32-34), professing:

All of the created order was made through the Son of God (1:2), making us His children (2:13). The Son of God was temporarily made lower than God's messengers to humanity—the angels (2:9)—by becoming a Son of Man (a Son of humanity) (2:6-7). He joined them in their struggle, as a brother (2:11-12, 17), though He rightfully had authority over them as their Father (2:13-14). He too was tempted (2:18). Sharing in the flesh of humanity, He tasted death for everyone (2:9), destroying the devil, who has power over death (2:14); delivering all those who are enslaved to the "fear of death" (2:15).

As a Son of Man and the Son of God, Jesus took up the role of High Priest so He could be an advocate for His children. After making purification for their sins (1:3), He ascended to heaven to sit at the position of authority (the right hand) until the day He comes again as the unique Son of God and Son of Man (2:17). Until that day, His children may struggle to "hold fast to their confession" in Him (2:1), but they can take comfort in their knowledge that nothing is outside the Son's control (2:8). He continues to join them in their pain (2:18), advocating on their behalf against the principalities and powers.

THE HEAVENLY CALLING

Pray that God would reveal His heavenly calling upon your life.

Read Hebrews 1:1–3:19. Reflect on 3:1–2.

In one to two sentences, summarize the point of Hebrews 1:1–2:18. Pay special attention to 1:1–2 and 2:3.

_____

_____

_____

_____

What do the "holy brothers [and sisters]" share? What are they to "consider" (3:1a)?

_____

_____

_____

_____

Jesus is called "the apostle and high priest of our confession" in 3:1b. "Apostle" literally means "sent one." Earlier, the author talked about Jesus and the angels being sent. Where are these occurrences? Jesus is called a "high priest" in earlier chapters as well; what is the context of these references?

_____

_____

_____

_____

What does it mean for Jesus to be "the apostle and high priest of our confession" (3:1b)? (Look for the other times "our confession" is used earlier in the book.)

_____

_____

_____

_____

_____

To whom is Jesus faithful? How was Jesus appointed (3:2)? (Read 1:1–4 to find the answer.)

_____

_____

_____

_____

Read Exodus 12. How was Moses "faithful in all God's house" (Heb 3:2)?

_____

_____

_____

_____

What is our calling? How can we discover it?

_____

_____

_____

_____

GOD'S HOUSE

Pray that God would reveal His faithfulness and how you can be more faithful to Him.

Read Hebrews 3:1–19. Reflect on 3:3–6.

Why is Jesus "counted worthy of more glory than Moses" (3:3)?

_____

_____

_____

In what ways is Jesus the "builder" of the house (3:3)? (Read 1:1–4 to find the answer.)

_____

_____

_____

God is also called the "builder" of the house in 3:4. What does this say about Jesus' relationship to God? (Hebrews 1:2 and 3:4 both use the term "all things"; this may explain Jesus' relationship to God.)

_____

_____

_____

_____

What are the "things that [Moses testified to that] were to [be] spoken later" (3:6a)? (Luke 24:13–27, especially verse 27, sheds some light on this.)

_____

_____

_____

"Over" what is Christ "faithful"? In what way is He "faithful" (3:6a)?

_____

_____

_____

What are the implications of us being "God's house" (3:6b)? (Note that the first plural, "us," is used here—meaning all of us.) Compare this verse to 1 Corinthians 3:16–17, where the "you" is also a plural ("you [all]").

_____

_____

_____

_____

What are we to hold fast to? What (or who) is our hope (Heb 3:6c)?

_____

_____

_____

How can we be more "faithful in all God's house," like Moses and Jesus are?

_____

_____

_____

HEARING GOD'S VOICE

Pray that God would speak to you.

Read Hebrews 3:1–19. Reflect on 3:7–12.

How does Hebrews 3:1–6 connect to 3:7a?

_____

_____

_____

_____

The Holy Spirit is talked about for the first time in the book in 3:7a. What is the Holy Spirit's function here?

_____

_____

_____

_____

The quote in Hebrews 3:7b–11 is from Psalm 95:7b–11. Read Psalm 95, which is a reflection upon Exodus 32. What is the primary theme of this psalm in its original context? What is the meaning of this psalm in the context of Hebrews?

_____

_____

_____

_____

Hebrews 3:12 begins with urgency—the Greek phrase is probably best expressed as "Look out!" What urgent matter does the author want us to "look out" for? Why is the author so concerned?

_____

_____

_____

_____

_____

What can we do to be more intentional ("look out" for) in our faith, and the faith of our other brothers and sisters in Christ?

_____

_____

_____

_____

_____

GOD'S COMMUNITY

Pray that God would help you to further realize the importance of His community.

Read Hebrews 3:1–19. Reflect on 3:13–19.

For how long are we to "exhort one another"? What are we to "exhort one another" in, and why?

_____

_____

_____

_____

Who is the "we" in 3:14a? What have "we" come to "share in"?

_____

_____

_____

_____

"Our confidence" is mentioned in 3:6. Why is it mentioned again here in 3:14b?

_____

_____

_____

_____

_____

Hebrews 3:14b says "we should hold our original confidence firm to the end." Hebrews 1:2 also talks about the end in its own way. What light does 1:2 shed on this verse?

_____

_____

_____

_____

_____

Psalm 95:7–8, quoted in Hebrews 3:15, is also quoted in 3:7–8. Why would the author emphasize this particular verse? What light does Hebrews 3:16–19 and Psalm 95 shed on this?

_____

_____

_____

_____

_____

How can you become more involved with God's community and have others exhort you to "hold fast to your confidence" in God?

_____

_____

_____

_____

_____

GOD'S REST

Pray that God would teach you about His rest.

Read Hebrews 1:1–4:16. Reflect on 4:1–2.

Summarize Hebrews 3 in a few sentences. How does it connect to Hebrews 4:1–16?

_____

_____

_____

_____

_____

What does it mean for us to "enter his rest" (4:1a)? What is God's rest?

_____

_____

_____

_____

What are we to fear? What is the result of us not fearing (4:1b)?

_____

_____

_____

_____

What is the good news? To whom else did the good news come? (See Heb 4:2a, Psa 95:7–11, and Exod 32.) What light does Hebrews 1:1–2 shed on 4:2a?

_____

_____

_____

_____

_____

Why did the message not benefit those who previously heard the good news (4:2)?

_____

_____

_____

_____

_____

How can God's followers be united (4:2b)? How can we strive toward entering God's rest together?

_____

_____

_____

_____

_____

RESTING IN WHO GOD IS

Pray that God would reveal to you the purpose and meaning of resting in Him.

Read Hebrews 1:1–4:16. Reflect on 4:3–10.

Summarize 4:1–2. Who enters God's rest (4:3)?

_____

_____

_____

_____

_____

The author quotes Psalm 95:11 in 4:3a—Read Psalm 95. Why do some people not enter God's rest? (See Heb 4:6.)

_____

_____

_____

_____

How do God's works, which have been "finished from the foundation of the world" (Heb 4:3b), connect to our rest in Him? (See Heb 4:4, which is a quote from Gen 2:2.)

_____

_____

_____

_____

The author quotes Psalm 95:11 again in Hebrews 4:5 to emphasize his point. Those who failed to enter God's rest are discussed in Hebrews 3:5–19 (compare Psa 95 and Exod 32). Why does God appoint "a certain day" for the Hebrews roaming in the wilderness to "hear his voice" (Heb 4:7a)? Are we also given a certain day to "hear his voice," and what day are we given? (See Psa 95:7–8, which is quoted in Heb 4:7b.)

_____

_____

_____

_____

In Hebrews 4:8, the author presents a theoretical situation—Joshua, Moses' predecessor as leader of Israel, giving rest to the Hebrews roaming in the wilderness. What is the author's conclusion about this theoretical situation?

_____

_____

_____

Is the Sabbath rest (resting on the seventh day, after laboring for six days) the only kind of rest the author is speaking about, or is there another kind of rest in view here (4:9–10)?

_____

_____

_____

How can we too enter God's rest? Would God have us rest more? What is the larger spiritual implication of resting in who God is and what Christ has done?

_____

_____

_____

THE WORD OF GOD

Pray that God would reveal the mystery of His Word.

Read Hebrews 1:1–4:16. Reflect on 4:11–13.

Summarize 4:1–10 in a couple of sentences.

_____

_____

_____

_____

What "rest" are we to strive to enter, and why (4:11)? (See 3:5–19.)

_____

_____

_____

_____

What is the Word of God? (See how God speaks creation into being in Gen 1, the prophetic word of God in Ezekiel 12:17–28, the word made flesh in John 1:1–4, 14–18, and the taught/received word in 1 Thessalonians 2:13–16 and James 1:21–27. It may also be helpful to run a search using Bible software for "word of God," followed by a search for "word of the Lord.")

_____

_____

_____

_____

What is the first way the author describes the word of God (Heb 4:12a)? What is the meaning of this description? What are the other four ways the author describes the word of God (4:12a–e)? (The first way is the principle behind the other four ways.)

_____

_____

_____

_____

_____

_____

_____

_____

Who is hidden from the sight of God (4:13a)? Who has to give account to God (4:13b)?

_____

_____

_____

_____

Are you striving to enter God's rest? Is the word of God living in your life? Do you feel accountable to God?

_____

_____

_____

_____

_____

OUR GREAT HIGH PRIEST— JESUS THE SON OF GOD

Pray that God would reveal His grace to you.

Read Hebrews 1:1–4:16. Reflect on 4:14–16.

Who is our great high priest, and how did He come to humanity
(4:14; compare 1:1–4)?

_____

_____

_____

_____

What should be our response to having a great high priest (4:14b)? (For more
information on high priests see Leviticus 23:26–32.)

_____

_____

_____

_____

What is "our confession" (Heb 4:14b)? (See 2:1 and 3:1b.) How do we hold fast to
our confession? (See 4:16.)

_____

_____

_____

_____

Can our high priest "sympathize with our weaknesses" and understand our "temptations" (4:15)? (Luke 4:1–13 illustrates Hebrews 4:15 well.)

_____

_____

_____

_____

_____

How can we "draw near to the throne of grace," and what is the result of us doing so (Heb 4:16)?

_____

_____

_____

_____

_____

How do we obtain "grace" (4:16)? Does the "grace" we are given just help us, or does it help others as well?

_____

_____

_____

_____

_____

_____

CONCLUSION

Grace is undeserved—more powerful than you or I. The Son of God gave up His deserved place in heaven to become the suffering and crucified Son of Man for us. He knows our weaknesses and the temptations we endure. We need to place our trust in Him, and (re)discover the power of His grace. May you "draw near to the throne of grace" and find peaceful rest in God, in the midst of even the most difficult of times.

HEBREWS 5–6

Pain is unavoidable and frequently makes life unbearable. When we are hurting we search for people who can sympathize with our weaknesses, trying to find a way to face the day. When we don't find someone who can help us in time, we often plummet into the pit of temptation. Crying out in the darkness, we search for answers.

The author of the book of Hebrews addressed these urgent problems with the urgency of the gospel. He commanded Christians to hold fast to their confession that the Son of God became flesh so that through His death He might destroy the one who has power over death, the devil (Heb 2:14; 4:14). Jesus sympathizes with our weaknesses because He too was tempted, but unlike us, Jesus did not sin (Heb 2:18; 4:15). We can find mercy and grace in our time of need by drawing near to the Son of God—our compassionate high priest, Jesus (Heb 4:15–16).

SON OF GOD BECOMES SON OF MAN

🤚 *Pray that God would reveal the message of the book of Hebrews to you.*

📄 *Read the whole book of Hebrews aloud while following the steps below.*

Underline and highlight key transition words like "but," "however" and "therefore." These types of phrases tell us when the author is contrasting something or drawing a conclusion.

In chapters 1–6, underline or highlight the phrases "Son of God," "Son of Man" and "high priest," and the words "Jesus," "flesh" "Christ," "confession," and "confidence." (You may want to use different colors.) Examining these words we see how the author's thoughts progress throughout the book.

Much of Hebrews 1:1–4:15 is building towards an eternal commandment in 4:16. What is this commandment? How does it offer you hope?

_____

_____

_____

_____

_____

_____

HOLD FAST HOPE

Pray that God would bring you hope in whatever struggles you are enduring.

Read Hebrews 3–4.

The author traces the Son of God coming into the world in Hebrews 1–2. Examine how the phrases "Son of God," "Son of Man," "Jesus," and "flesh" are used in tandem. This helps us understand the unique Son of God's divinely appointed role as the Son of Man. Whose role is this contrasted with in chapters 1–2?

_____

_____

_____

What does 3:6 tell us about Christ? What is God's house?

_____

_____

_____

_____

With what you know about God's household in mind, reflect upon the phrases that use the words "confession" and "confidence"?

_____

_____

_____

_____

_____

What is the Son of God called in 4:15? What is the purpose of His new vocation? (Compare 2:17–18.)

_____

_____

_____

_____

What are we commanded to do in 4:16? (Compare 4:14.) The Son of God temporarily gave up His role as co-creator of the universe—the highest appointment in all of the heavens—to suffer with us. Take hope because the Son of God has placed hope in you.

_____

_____

_____

_____

TEMPORAL PRIESTS, ETERNAL PRIEST

Pray that God would show you what it means for Jesus to be our high priest.

Read Hebrews 5–6. Reflect on 5:1–6.

Hebrews 5:1–3 supports the statements in 4:14–16. How is a high priest chosen? What two things is every high priest appointed to do?

_____

_____

_____

_____

According to 5:2–3, why can a high priest relate to our weaknesses? What two sacrifices does a high priest make? (Compare Leviticus 4:4, 9:7 and 16:6.)

_____

_____

_____

_____

How was the high priest appointed (5:4)? Who was Aaron? If you don't know, look "Aaron" up in a concordance, or search for him on Biblia.com. Be sure to read what God says about Aaron in Exodus 28:1.

_____

_____

_____

How was Christ appointed for His position (Heb 5:5)? What was said to Him when He was appointed? Hebrews 5:6b is a quote from Psalm 2:7. (Psalm 2:7 is also quoted in Hebrews 1:5.) How is Hebrews 1:1–5 connected to Hebrews 5:5? Read and reflect upon Psalm 2 and what it tells us about the Son of God's role.

_____

_____

_____

_____

_____

What are the two ways the author describes Christ in Hebrews 5:6? Hebrews 5:6 is a quote from Psalm 110:4. Read Psalm 110, and reflect upon what it tells us about Christ's role, especially in light of the beginning of the book of Hebrews. (What it means for Jesus to be "after the order of Melchizedek" will be explained later in the book.)

_____

_____

_____

_____

_____

There is a subtle, but important, contrast in Hebrews 5:1–6 between temporal priests, like Aaron, and Christ's eternal priesthood (5:6). Christ's eternal priesthood is unique, like His role as the Son of God. What are the effects of this priesthood upon our lives now and in the future?

_____

_____

_____

_____

JESUS IN THE FLESH

Pray that God would reveal to you the purpose of Jesus' suffering and your own.

Read Hebrews 5. Reflect on 5:7–10.

What did Jesus do "in the days of his flesh" (5:7a)? (Take note of the action words in this verse.) What parts of Jesus' prayer habits can you apply to your life?

_____

_____

_____

_____

_____

Why were Jesus' prayers heard (5:7b)? Even though Jesus' prayers were heard, He was not spared from death. (Compare Luke 22:39–46.)

_____

_____

_____

How did Jesus learn when He was in the flesh here on earth (Heb 5:8)? (The author makes a contrast here—"although he was a son.") Jesus was a "son of God"—His unique one—and even He had to learn obedience.

_____

_____

_____

_____

What is Jesus the source of in 5:9? How did He become the source? (Underline 5:9—it is one of the most important verses in the entire book.) The author elaborates upon this in light of Jesus' vocation, reiterating what is said in 5:6.

_____

_____

_____

_____

_____

God can be influenced through our prayers, but sometimes no matter what we pray, God has appointed a path for us that we must learn to obediently follow. We don't like the idea that through suffering we learn to follow God, or that God would allow us to suffer to learn obedience. But in an imperfect world, that is the way things work. The more you follow God, the harder living in this world will be. Let's not forget that the Son of God is here for us when it _really_ hurts. With Him who has overcome death, we can face death itself with confidence.

MILK, NOT SOLID FOOD

Ask God to help you digest solid spiritual food.

Read Hebrews 5. Reflect upon 5:11–14.

Hebrews 5:11–14 is the application of 4:14–5:10 for the community being addressed. Why is it difficult for the author to explain things to the Christians being addressed?

_____

_____

_____

_____

_____

Where does the author expect his audience to be in their spiritual journey by now (5:12)? Where are they instead? What kind of food do these Christians need? What kind of food should they be eating (5:12)? What attributes describe those living on milk (5:13)? (The "word of righteousness" is the prophetic message the Christians have heard about Jesus that leads them to live rightly before God.)

_____

_____

_____

_____

_____

_____

What do mature Christians, who eat solid spiritual food, possess (5:14)? Do these things come easily? What is the ultimate result of living on solid food?

_____

_____

_____

_____

_____

Has much of God's community today also become "dull of hearing"? Could the things said in 5:11–14 be said of many Christians today? Should it be said? Are you living on milk or solid food? What could you do to live on more solid food?

_____

_____

_____

_____

_____

_____

DOCTRINE 101

Pray that God would teach you about the essential doctrines of our faith.

Read Hebrews 6. Reflect on 6:1–3.

What does the speaker wish for Christians to do (6:1)? What are the five things the author lists as elementary doctrines in 6:1–2?

_____

_____

_____

_____

_____

Check out the doctrines mentioned in 6:1–2 by looking up these key words/ phrases in a concordance or searching for them on Biblia.com: "repentance," "washings," "laying on of hands," "resurrection of the dead," and "eternal judgment." (Look primarily at the New Testament occurrences.)

Reflect upon these doctrines and the importance of them to your life. How does knowing about these doctrines help you to face each day with new hope?

_____

_____

_____

_____

_____

FALL AWAY OR FALL INTO GOD

 Pray that God would teach you how to better follow Him.

 Read Hebrews 6. Reflect on 6:4–18.

The urgency of the message of the author becomes crystal clear in these verses. Enlightenment in Hebrews 6:4 has to do with understanding the gospel. What are the other four previous experiences of the person who has *now* "fallen away" (6:4–6)? The Greek word "falling away" (*parapipto*, παραπίπτω) means to "fall beside" or "go astray." The type of person being described understands the gospel and followed Jesus for a while before indignantly turning away from Christ. They are now continually faithless and disobedient, even though they once repented from their sin. They have seen the light and walked away. The first repentance is discussed in Hebrews 6:1–2.

_____

_____

_____

_____

Why is it "impossible" *for us* (not God) to "renew again ... to repentance" those who have "fallen away" (4:6)? ("Renew again" better encompasses the idea of the original Greek.) All repentance has to come through Christ. There may not be an opportunity to turn back again (e.g., Heb 12:7). Those who "fall away" are metaphorically "crucifying the Son of God to their own harm and holding him up to contempt" (4:6). They are making a mockery of Him like those who physically crucified Him. They know the truth and yet have turned away—so they are in league with the forces working against God. You are on God's team or playing for the enemy. The enemy killed Jesus and celebrates His death; Christians celebrate His resurrected life. This is what the author means by the parable in 6:7–8:

"For ground that drinks the rain that comes often upon it, and brings forth vegetation usable to those people for whose sake it is also cultivated, shares a blessing from God."

Meaning: A person that has listened to and obeyed God's guidance performs good godly works helpful to others and God, and receives a blessing from God for doing so.

"But if it produces thorns and thistles, it is worthless and near to a curse, whose end is for burning.

Meaning: If someone regularly does evil things, they have a slight chance of coming back to God, but not much—they will perish if they don't turn back towards God and start doing good works.

Of what does the author feel sure (6:9)? Why is the author so sure (6:10)? What things "belong to salvation"? (Think specifically of 6:7–8.)

_____

_____

_____

_____

_____

What is desired of each of us (6:11)? Why should we not become "sluggish" (6:12)? (Reflect upon this in light of 6:1–8 and the end drawing near.) In 6:13–14, the author supports this view on the basis of God's promise to Abraham, quoting from Genesis 22:17. How does God swearing a promise "by himself" relate to the rest of Hebrews 6 (6:15–17)?

_____

_____

_____

_____

What are the "two unchangeable things" that make it "impossible for God to lie" (6:18)? Why should we be strongly encouraged?

_____

_____

_____

_____

_____

What can you do to make sure you follow God's will? What changes can you make to ensure that you bear good fruit?

_____

_____

_____

_____

_____

AN ANCHOR FOR THE SOUL

Pray that God would reveal to you how you can be anchored.

Read Hebrews 6. Reflect upon 6:19–20.

What is "sure and steadfast" and an "anchor of the soul" (6:19)?

_____

_____

_____

_____

Jesus metaphorically enters into the inner place behind the curtain in the temple, where God is in His "holy of holies" (6:19). Whose forerunner is He (6:20)? What has Jesus now become? How long will He hold this position?

_____

_____

_____

_____

How does Jesus' position directly affect your life?

_____

_____

_____

_____

CONCLUSION

In the midst of a hectic life that might at times feel hopeless, may you realize that God has sent His Son to be an eternal advocate for you. Hope exists in Jesus.

Jesus, the high priest, has pleaded your case and won because He paid for your mistakes. He has the evidence and He is the reason for a positive verdict. May you serve Him until the end, making Him the anchor of your soul.

HEBREWS 7–8

Economic failure and job losses have become commonplace. Painful circumstances are tearing away at the cultural, church, and family ties that hold us together. It has become hard to see Jesus. But what if times were worse? What if we were waiting for God to eternally redeem us as well? This was the case before the Son of God came to earth.

After addressing many of the pressing issues of the first century AD (and likewise today), the author discusses Jesus' priesthood. We must hold fast to the ultimate hope: The Son of God who became Son of Man, Jesus (Heb 1:5; 2:16). He relates to our finite struggles because He too endured pain and temptation (2:14–18). But the Son of God doesn't quit there; He alters the course of the infinite by becoming our high priest and the sacrifice that makes us one with God again.

HIGH PRIEST OF THE PAST, HIGH PRIEST OF THE PRESENT

Pray that God would reveal the purpose of Jesus' high priesthood to you.

Read the entire book of Hebrews aloud in one setting.

Underline "high priest" each time it occurs. Pay attention to how the author compares and contrasts Jesus as the high priest with other priests.

Reflect on 5:1–8. What does the vocation of a priest entail? (List the four things the author describes.)

1. _____

2. _____

3. _____

4. _____

Aaron, Moses' brother, was the first high priest after the Israelites left Egypt. Under the guidance of God, Moses decided how religious practice was to be conducted in the wilderness and eventually in the promised land. Aaron and his sons, who were from the tribe of Levi, were in charge of making sure the people worshiped God correctly. They also interceded between God and the Israelites by offering sacrifices that symbolized payment for their wrongdoings. But the system had a fatal flaw: the priests weren't perfect (Heb 5:2–3), which made the sacrificial system imperfect and temporary. How is Jesus the same as other priests? How is He different?

_____

_____

_____

_____

What sacrifice did Jesus make? How does His sacrifice alter your view of God and affect your life?

_____

_____

_____

_____

_____

CONSIDER JESUS

Pray that God would show you more areas of your life that Jesus can enter.

Read Hebrews 2–4. Reflect on 2:14–18.

Why does Jesus help us? What did Jesus have to do to become a faithful high priest? What was His role before becoming a high priest? (See Heb 1:1–14.)

_____

_____

_____

_____

Reflect on Hebrews 3:1–6. What type of calling do we have (3:1)? Jesus is an apostle (one sent from God) and a high priest (someone who intercedes between people and God). What is our confession?

_____

_____

_____

_____

Reflect on Hebrews 4:11–16. From where did Jesus come (4:14)? What can Jesus do that He previously could not do before He took on flesh (4:15)? What are we commanded to do (4:14, 16)?

_____

_____

_____

_____

What can you do to better align your life with God's calling?

_____

_____

_____

_____

_____

The Son of God can sympathize with our weaknesses because He became like us. Take hope in having an advocate between you and God who knows what it is like to struggle, hurt, and be tempted. Hold fast to your faith in, and obedience to, the Son of God, our eternal high priest.

CHOSEN BY GOD

Pray that God would help you understand Jesus' vocation and your calling.

Read Hebrews 5–6.

Rather than being chosen by people to be a high priest like Aaron (5:1), Jesus was appointed by God to be a high priest after the order of Melchizedek (5:5, 10).

Reflect on 6:13–20. God's promise to us, like His promise to Abraham, is guaranteed with an oath (6:19–20). This oath involves God appointing Jesus as a high priest (7:17, 21), as well as Jesus entering the inner sanctuary behind the curtain in the temple, where God is in His "holy of holies" (6:19). The sacrifice was offered before God Himself in the heavenly temple, which was represented on earth by the tabernacle and, ultimately, the temple in Jerusalem.

Hebrews 6–8 draws from the story of Abraham (called Abram at the time) and his 318 trained men who defeat King Chedorlaomer and a coalition of other kings. These kings had invaded the city of Sodom, where Abram's nephew Lot was living. After Abram defeats the kings, the kings of Sodom and Salem come out to thank him. Read the rest of the story in Genesis 14:17–24. Pay special attention to the actions of the King of Salem, Melchizedek. Salem is where Jerusalem was eventually built.

How does Melchizedek's blessing of Abraham (Gen 14:17–24) relate to God's promise to Abraham in Genesis 15?

_____

_____

_____

_____

_____

God has a plan. The story of Abraham and Melchizedek in Genesis 14–15 provides the backdrop for the Christ to come, according to the author of Hebrews. What is God doing today that may provide a backdrop for His future plans? (Think about what the Son of God is currently doing for us.)

_____

_____

_____

_____

_____

_____

WITHOUT BEGINNING OR END OF DAYS

🤚 *Pray that God reveals to you the greatness of His Son and the purpose of tithing.*

📄 *Read Hebrews 7–8.*

What did Abraham apportion to Melchizedek (7:2a, 4)? Should we apportion the same to Jesus?

_____

_____

_____

_____

The Hebrew word *Melechi* (מלכי) means "my king" and *sedeq* (צדק) means "righteous;" thus Melchizedek's name means "my king is righteous." Since Melchizedek is also a priest of the Most High God, we can infer that his name should be interpreted "my king [the Most High God] is righteous." His very name expresses the idea that the Most High God is king. Melchizedek was the "king of Salem"; Salem has the same consonants as the verb that means "to bring peace, wholeness, or completion" (*shalam*, שלם). In addition to these attributes, in what other way is Melchizedek like the Son of God (7:3)?

_____

_____

_____

_____

What is the difference between those in the priestly office of Levi and Melchizedek (7:5–6a)? What did Melchizedek do for Abraham (7:6b)?

_____

_____

_____

_____

For one person to bless another during Old Testament times, they had to have a superior status. Melchizedek is superior to Abraham because he is both a priest and a king. The author of Hebrews also believed the descendants of Levi were "in the loins of Abraham" when he was blessed by Melchizedek (7:10). Thus, for the author, they too are inferior to Melchizedek and those in his priestly and kingly order (7:7–9).

Why is Jesus not part of the Levitical priesthood (7:13–14)? How did Jesus become a high priest in the likeness of Melchizedek (Heb 7:15–17; compare Psa 110:4)? Was the law about priesthood changed when Jesus became a priest (Heb 7:11–12, 18–19)?

_____

_____

_____

_____

Jesus is a better hope than the Old Testament Law (7:18–19) because He helps us personally draw near to God. He has become a priest by the power of His indestructible life and His anointing by God the Father (7:16–17). Do the finite things of this world seem to matter less to you when you reflect upon the indestructible, eternal person of Jesus?

_____

_____

_____

_____

PERFECT PRIEST FOREVER

Pray that God would show you the strength and power of Jesus' priesthood.

Read Hebrews 7–8.

What is the difference between Jesus' priesthood and the priesthood of the Levites (7:20–21)? (Hebrews 7:21b is a citation from Psalm 110:4.)

_____

_____

_____

_____

_____

Jesus' priesthood guarantees a better covenant than that of Abraham (Gen 14–15) and Moses. How long will Jesus hold His priesthood (Heb 7:23–24)? What is Jesus able to do because of His priesthood (7:25)? A covenant is an ancient contract. The covenants between God and Abraham, God and Moses, and God the Father and Jesus all involve God promising He will do something, with the expectation that God's people will respond a particular way. How is the covenant between God the Father and Jesus different than God's covenants with Abraham and Moses?

_____

_____

_____

_____

_____

_____

What are the five ways Jesus is described in 7:26?

1. _____

_____

2. _____

_____

3. _____

_____

4. _____

_____

5. _____

_____

Why did the author chose to include these five descriptions? (Compare the attributes of Jesus and those of the Levitical priests listed in 7:26–28.)

_____

_____

_____

Jesus can perfect us in our weaknesses. His abilities are beyond those of the weak priests of past. The Son of God has altered history. How can we join Him in bringing change to our world?

_____

_____

_____

_____

THE POINT OF HEBREWS

Pray that God would show you how sending His Son is different from His other acts.

Read Hebrews 8.

This is one of the few places in the Bible where the author says, "Now here is the point." What is the author of Hebrews conveying here (8:1–2)?

_____

_____

_____

_____

_____

What was every high priest appointed to do (8:3)? What do the priests on earth offer, and whom do they serve (8:4–5a)? Why was Moses asked to make things for the sanctuary as he was "instructed … on the mountain" (8:5b)? (Hebrews 8:5b is a quote from Exodus 25:40.)

_____

_____

_____

_____

_____

_____

What covenant did Moses represent (Heb 8:6a)? What covenant does Jesus'
ministry embody (8:6b)? What are the "better promises" mentioned in
Hebrews 8:7? (See Heb 7:15–22.)

_____

_____

_____

_____

_____

Jesus has given us a new and better covenant. How should we respond to
this covenant?

_____

_____

_____

_____

_____

A NEW CONTRACT

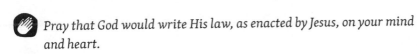

 Pray that God would write His law, as enacted by Jesus, on your mind and heart.

Read Hebrews 8.

Hebrews 8:8–12 is a quotation from Jeremiah 31:31–34. Read Jeremiah 30–31. This prophetic oracle was originally addressed to God's people who had been taken into slavery in Babylon by Nebuchadnezzar in 587 BC. The land and possessions of God's people were seized, and their king was dethroned. The people then endured the pain of marching across the ancient Near East as slaves. In the midst of this seemingly hopeless situation, Jeremiah offered the prophecy in Jeremiah 30–31. The prophecy promised God's people redemption, and God personally declared that He would do what He originally asked of them in Deuteronomy 6:4–6. God will be the primary actor in this "new covenant." He is the issuer and signer of this new contract.

What is the difference between the "new covenant" and the "old covenant"? (Compare Jeremiah 31:31–34 with Deuteronomy 6:4–6, looking for specific examples. Think of these examples in terms of Jesus.) How does God begin His "new covenant," according to the author of Hebrews?

_____

_____

_____

_____

_____

_____

_____

_____

How is the old covenant "obsolete" (Heb 8:13)? If the old covenant is "obsolete," should we still read the old covenant laws in Exodus, Leviticus, Numbers, and Deuteronomy? Has the old covenant been completely set aside, or has the arrival of Jesus just seriously reworked it?

_____

_____

_____

_____

_____

_____

What does our contract (covenant) with God now look like?

_____

_____

_____

_____

_____

_____

ONCE AND FOR ALL

👏 *Pray that God would show you the reason for Jesus' sacrifice.*

📄 *Read Hebrews 7–9.*

Hebrews 7–8 serves as a backdrop to the ideas in Hebrews 9. Why does the author go into such a detailed description of God's earthly dwelling?

_____

_____

_____

_____

What is the difference between the earthly priesthood and way of worship (9:1–10), and the way that Jesus establishes (9:11–28)?

_____

_____

_____

_____

What did Jesus do "once and for all" (9:26)? Why was the Son of God offered to God the Father as a sacrifice (9:27–28)?

_____

_____

_____

_____

_____

What is the significance of Jesus being both the priest and the sacrifice? How does Jesus' role as priest and sacrifice in God's miraculous story of redemption change our position with God?

_____

_____

_____

_____

_____

_____

CONCLUSION

With an ordinary priest, our sins would be forgiven, but the change would only be temporal, since we would inevitably sin again. With the Son of God as our priest and sacrifice, we are eternally forgiven. With Jesus, we can reach the heavens and as members of His new covenant bring a little heaven to earth. May you see Jesus transform your life and the lives of those around you. May you take hope in the fact that your situation, as dire as it may be, is only temporal. Life in Jesus is eternal.

HEBREWS 9–10

Four years ago, I was broken and hurting. For months, I returned to the same rock to pray. I prayed and prayed, but heard no answer. Then one day, God showed up. He offered me a chance to refinance. I was given the chance to renew our old contract under new terms—to learn again how to set aside my selfishness and live selflessly.

In the first century AD, those who first heard the words of the book of Hebrews were in a similar situation. For many, the state of affairs was worst. They had endured pain and suffering, and they needed direction (Heb 10:32–39). They needed a new mortgage, but one offered by someone much more powerful that your ordinary loan guy—their refinancing needed to be permanent. In these next few studies, we will learn what God's new contract with us is all about, who is involved, and how we should respond.

AN OLD CONTRACT WITH A NEW ADDENDUM

Pray that God would show you why He made a new covenant.

Read Hebrews 6–13 aloud in one setting.

A covenant is an ancient contract. Underline "covenant" each time it occurs in Hebrews 7–13. What is the difference between the first, old covenant and the second, new covenant?

_____

_____

_____

_____

Reflect on Hebrews 8:1–13. Hebrews 8:8–12 is a quotation of Jeremiah 31:31–34. Read Deuteronomy 6:4–6, which Jeremiah 31:31–34 echoes, and underline the pronouns "I" and "you" in these verses. What was the difference between the passages?

_____

_____

_____

_____

_____

God finds fault in the first covenant, in the priests who represent God's people (8:8a), and by extension Israel and Judah (8:8b). They didn't uphold their end of the contract—they failed to follow God. The covenant is flawed because people are flawed. We are all flawed. God could walk away, but He doesn't (8:9). He creates a new contract, where He is the guarantor. In this contract, the people "shall not teach" each other about the Lord; instead "they shall all know" Him (8:11).

Why is the first covenant ready to vanish away? Does "obsolete" mean "no longer valid" or "out of date"?

_____

_____

_____

_____

If the old covenant is invalid, then what God said would also be void, which is not the case. The new covenant uses nearly the same words as the old. However, the new covenant no longer relies on the people, now that God is the guarantor. Christ's sacrifice is how He enacts the covenant. Could it be that this new contract is an addendum to the old one? In what ways is the first contract still valid? What parts of it are vanishing away?

_____

_____

_____

_____

Should we rethink how our relationship with God functions in light of the new covenant?

_____

_____

_____

RESTRICTED AREAS AND OPEN ACCESS

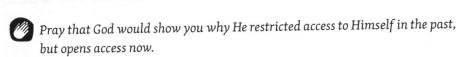 *Pray that God would show you why He restricted access to Himself in the past, but opens access now.*

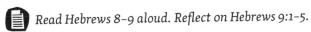 *Read Hebrews 8–9 aloud. Reflect on Hebrews 9:1–5.*

The blueprint for the earthly place of holiness (Heb 9:1), called the tabernacle, was given in Exodus 25–27.

Reflect on Hebrews 9:3–13. Only the high priest was allowed to enter God's presence in the Most Holy Place. Once there, the high priest burned incense perpetually upon the golden altar (Heb 9:4a; Exod 30:1–10). He did so not because God wanted a room that smelled like a glade plug-in, but because it reminded the people that they were in a holy place (Exod 30:8). The high priest also poured the blood of the sin offering upon the altar once a year. This symbolized the purification of God's people and the confirmation and revitalization of His relationship with them.

Was God's presence everywhere, or was it restricted to certain places at chosen times? The ark of the covenant symbolized God's very presence (Heb 9:4b; Lev 16:1–2). Atop the ark was the mercy seat, with two cherubim above it (Heb 9:5; Exod 25:22). Where could the high priest go that regular priests cannot (Heb 9:6–7)?

_____

_____

_____

_____

_____

_____

What did the high priest take with him into the Most Holy Place and why (Heb 9:7)? Why were the holy places closed to non-priests (9:8)? What does this restricted access area symbolize (9:9a)? What cannot be perfected by the old arrangement (9:9b–10)?

_____

_____

_____

_____

_____

Christ changed everything. What's different now (9:11–13)? How was the new covenant established (9:12b)? What did it secure (9:12c)? What's dead (9:13c)? Who's alive (9:13c)?

_____

_____

_____

_____

_____

What can we take into God's holy place in heaven someday? What can we _not_ take?

_____

_____

_____

_____

_____

CHRIST'S EXPENSE AND OUR INHERITANCE

Pray that God would show you the meaning and power of His new covenant.

Read Hebrews 9. Reflect on Hebrews 9:15–17.

Who is the mediator of the new covenant (Heb 9:13–15)? Whose death is in picture in Hebrews 9:15–17, and what is its effect?

_____

_____

_____

_____

_____

We have a future inheritance and a current one. If eternal life begins now, what is our future inheritance? Must we work for *it* or *toward* it?

_____

_____

_____

_____

_____

_____

_____

The word often translated as "will" (*diatheke*; διαθήκη) in Hebrews 9:16–17 is the same word translated as "covenant" throughout the passage. When does a covenant take effect (9:16–17)?

_____

_____

_____

_____

_____

In light of this, why did Christ die? How did Christ's death change your standing with God?

_____

_____

_____

_____

_____

_____

_____

_____

A CONTRACT THAT REQUIRES A DEATH, BUT CREATES LIFE

Pray that God would teach you why Jesus died.

Read Hebrews 9. Reflect on Hebrews 9:18–28.

How was the first covenant inaugurated and how were the things used for worship purified (9:18–22)? What book is sprinkled by Moses (9:19b)? (Hebrews 9:20 is a quote from Exodus 24:8; read Exodus 24 to find which book is sprinkled.) What does the shedding of blood accomplish (9:22b)?

_____

_____

_____

_____

_____

What are the "copies of the heavenly things" mentioned in Hebrews 9:23a? (Read 9:2–5 to find out.) What are the heavenly things and the better sacrifice (9:23b)? (Check out 9:24.)

_____

_____

_____

_____

_____

Why isn't Christ offered repeatedly, like the animals previously (9:25–26a)? What did He do instead and what is the effect of His action (9:26b)?

_____

_____

_____

_____

_____

_____

Christ will be back. This time He is coming not to deal with our sins, because He has already taken care of them, but to permanently save us from this fallen world. Until then, we must wait (9:27–28). While we are waiting for Christ to return, what can we do to follow God closely?

_____

_____

_____

_____

_____

_____

THIS COVENANT WILL LAST

Pray that Jesus' words would transform you.

Read Hebrews 9–10. Reflect on Hebrews 10:1–10.

Why, under the law, were sacrifices continually offered (9:1–2)? The sacrifices in view in Hebrews 10:1–4 occurred once a year on the Day of Atonement (Lev 16:15–22).

_____

_____

_____

Hebrews 10:5–7 records Christ paraphrasing Psalm 40:6–8. This is not recorded in the Gospels, so we are getting a unique quote from Christ here. What does Christ add to Psalm 40:6–8? Why does He do so (10:9)? (Think about the difference in the two covenants discussed earlier in our study.) Again, the word translated as "will" in 10:10 is the same word translated as "covenant" elsewhere in Hebrews 9–10.

_____

_____

_____

Through what covenant are we sanctified (progressively made set-apart for God) (10:10)? How is the covenant made? How long will it last? How does this change your standing with God and affect your day-to-day routine?

_____

_____

_____

TKO: GOD WINS

Pray that you would find your place in God's war for humanity.

Read Hebrews 10. Reflect on Hebrews 10:11–18.

What did every priest in the first century AD do (10:11)? What did Christ do after making His sacrifice (10:12–13)?

_____

_____

_____

_____

_____

The right hand of God is the position of favor and power. When an enemy becomes one's footstool, they have submitted their authority, willingly or by force. In this case, the devil and those who crucified Christ are the ones who played the fool—He is the one now in authority. He is in the position of power at the right hand of God, and they are in the position of submission as His footstool.

What did Christ's offering accomplish (10:14)? What bears witness to the offering (10:15)? If the Spirit is present, are any parts of the Trinity missing? What does this indicate about the way God takes back the power that is rightfully His?

_____

_____

_____

_____

_____

What is being forgiven in 10:18, and what is the result of this forgiveness? How are our lives affected by Christ's momentous act and unexpected victory? What remains the same? What changes? How can we join God's fight?

_____

_____

_____

_____

_____

_____

THE CURTAIN IS RIPPED AND THE WAY IS REVEALED

Pray that God would reveal to you what it means to live a life of grace.

Read Hebrews 10. Reflect on Hebrews 10:19–31.

What should we have confidence to do now that Christ has obtained victory over death and evil (Heb 10:19)? Are we entering earth or heaven (10:19)? (Look back at Part VI, Lesson 2.)

_____

_____

_____

The curtain mentioned in Hebrews 10:20 separated non-priests from God's holy presence inside the tabernacle (Exod 26). Three of the gospels record this curtain being torn when Christ died (Matt 27:51; Mark 15:38; Luke 23:45). The curtain is also mentioned in Hebrews 6:19 and 9:3. Why should we, who have fallen short of God's glory and will, have confidence to enter God's holy presence (10:20)?

_____

_____

_____

Who is the great priest mentioned in 10:21? (Read Heb 6–7.)

_____

_____

_____

What are the three things we need to do when approaching God (10:22)? Do these things apply to us today?

_____

_____

_____

_____

_____

Why should we hold fast to our confession (10:23)? Our hope is in Christ an eternal inheritance—a new life that begins now.

_____

_____

_____

_____

_____

What are the three things 10:24–26 says we should do? Why should we do them (10:26–27)?

_____

_____

_____

_____

Christ didn't die so we could go on sinning, but so that we could stop sinning (10:26). He doesn't want us to live under judgment any longer (10:27); He wants us to live in the Spirit of grace (10:29). We have freedom to live a life of helping and caring for others—like Christ did when He was here on earth. We have no reason to walk away (10:30–31). We must follow God until the end because He is the living God (10:31) who allowed for His own Son's blood to be spilled for us (10:29).

A HARD STRUGGLE

Pray that God would show you how to endure in the midst of turmoil and pain.

Read Hebrews 10. Reflect on Hebrews 10:32–39.

What happened to the author's audience in the "former days" (10:32–33)? When did it happen? For whom were they compassionate (10:34a)? What did they accept and why (10:34b)?

_____

_____

_____

What does the author of Hebrews ask the audience to do (10:35)? Their great reward is Christ and eternal life with Him. What will happen if they endure (10:36)? Is the same true for us today?

_____

_____

_____

Why is the author so confident in his resolve? Hebrews 10:37–38 echoes and combines Isaiah 26:20, Haggai 2:6, and Habakkuk 2:3–4. These lines were originally about God restoring His people from foreign rule, but here they are about Christ spiritually restoring them on the day He returns. The foreign rule in view here is selfishness, driven by the devil (Heb 2:14).

_____

_____

_____

_____

Align yourself with a group: "those who shrink back and are destroyed"; or "those who have faith and persevere." Destruction is inevitable for those who choose not to follow Christ because any other choice is the devil's road (2:14). And the devil's road ends in destruction—he's on the fast train to Hades. But we all have a choice and choice is a gift. And we can all endure because Christ and His church are with us. Prayer, reading His Word and being surrounded by a strong group of Christians will help us endure any and all circumstances.

CONCLUSION

It is easier not to care than to care. Yet, the author of Hebrews was confident that the church could be convinced to help those being unjustly victimized by people in power. To paraphrase the author's thoughts: "You should care and you can endure. Just remember who Christ is and what He did for you. And bear in mind that you have endured worse. Then, make a decision—persevere or be destroyed." There is a difference between meandering away from Christ and completely walking away. Those who defiantly oppose Christ, claiming He doesn't exist or isn't the savior, will be destroyed. Those who meander won't, if they believe in Christ. But they are putting themselves and others at risk because all other paths belong to the devil (2:14). If you fall short, don't walk away from your faith; let Christ pick you up. He will be gracious. May you see that you have the gift of choice and time. You have time to choose Christ's new contract.

HEBREWS 11

No, not chapter 11 as in U.S. bankruptcy. While Hebrews 11 isn't going to solve financial problems, it presents examples of how to live *in faith*, no matter what your circumstances. The author of Hebrews makes faith tangible for his audience who is suffering (Heb 6:4; 11:8). The author responds to their situation with the message of "hold fast" (6:18; 10:23, 32–33), like a whole host of people before them did.

When we feel that we can't see God at work, the author of Hebrews tells us to look to followers of God from times past as an example. If we look hard enough, God will eventually surface. Hebrews 11 provides a plethora of real-life examples that address the book's most pressing question, "How can we have faith in the midst of pain and suffering?" In these next studies, we will examine what the author of Hebrews said to a community that was struggling to have faith. We will learn what faith is, how to have it, and where to place it.

AN OLD CONTRACT WITH A NEW ADDENDUM

Pray that God would bring to your mind past events that He brought you through.

Read Hebrews 10:32–12:2 aloud in one setting. Reflect on Hebrews 10:32–39.

In 10:32, what word is used to describe how the community being addressed came to faith? What does the author's choice of this word tell us about the process of coming to faith in Christ? (Do you have to be told to believe? Does it involve learning something? If so, what else does 10:32–39 seem to indicate is in the mix?)

_____

_____

_____

_____

_____

_____

What happened after the community came to faith (10:32–33a)? Take special note of the verbs (the action words) used.

_____

_____

_____

_____

_____

With whom did the community partner (10:33b) and why (10:34a)? What did they accept (10:34b), and what word is used to describe how they accepted it? Would you be able to have the same attitude if what happened to this Christian community happened to you? In this regard, does "joy" mean "happiness"? Is there a better way to describe "joy"? (Read Habakkuk 3:17–19 for an example of true joy.)

_____

_____

_____

_____

_____

_____

In Hebrews 10:35, after recalling what this Christian community has endured, what does the author call them to do, and why does he do so?

_____

_____

_____

_____

_____

Based on 10:36, what appears to be the ultimate goal? (The goal involves two things.)

_____

_____

_____

_____

_____

How long must we endure (10:37–38)? Who is coming for us? (Hebrews 10:37–38 is a combination of Isaiah 26:20, Haggai 2:6, and Habakkuk 2:3-4.)

_____

_____

_____

_____

_____

What group do we *not* want to be affiliated with (10:39)? Why?

_____

_____

_____

_____

_____

Like the author of Hebrews calls his community to do, think back upon all the times God has helped you endure difficult circumstances. Now think of painful events in which you didn't see God. Do you see how God acted in those circumstances now? Is it possible that in your current situation, God is acting and you don't even know it? Maybe you don't see Him because you simply aren't looking.

WHAT WE DON'T SEE, WE CAN STILL UNDERSTAND

Pray that God would help you understand and define faith, and then apply it to your life.

Read Hebrews 10:32–11:2 aloud in one setting. Reflect on Hebrews 11:1–2.

Underline the verbs in these two verses:

> Now faith is the assurance of things hoped for, the conviction of things not seen. For by it the people of old received their commendation. (Heb 11:1–2 ESV)

What is faith? If we have faith, what can we receive? What can we offer?

_____

_____

_____

_____

_____

Does faith have to do with more than just an affirmation of something? Is it both a personal decision and an outwardly expressed act?

_____

_____

_____

_____

_____

Does faith convict us and change us? If faith involves us affirming God, and God commending us, does faith then revolve around a relationship? What can you do to make this relationship more recognizable by others? How should this relationship function? In externalizing your relationship with God, you will come to a better understanding of what faith in Him really means.

_____

_____

_____

_____

_____

_____

IN FAITH AND WITHOUT FAITH

Pray that God would teach you what you can do with faith, and how you are inhabited without it.

Read Hebrews 10:39–11:7 aloud in one setting. Reflect on Hebrews 11:3–7.

Underline all the verbs in the following verse:

> By faith we understand that the universe was created by the word of God, so that what is seen was not made out of things that are visible. (Heb 11:3 ESV)

Read Genesis 1–2, John 1:1–4, Colossians 1:15–22, and 1 Corinthians 8:6. What are the effects of Christ being involved in creation? In light of Hebrews 11:3, how does Christ being a co-creator of the world relate to us acting in faith? For the author of Hebrews, it is not that we act in our own faith, but that we place our faith in Christ, who acts through us. We are to hand over our burdens, worries, cares, and pain to Him.

_____

_____

_____

Read Hebrews 11:4 and Genesis 4. What is so significant about Abel's act? Does it foreshadow a future sacrifice? What does the author of Hebrews mean when he says that Abel "still speaks"? This verse doesn't speak to an ability Abel had, like a positive outlook on life. Rather, Abel is commended for looking to God as the object of his belief.

_____

_____

_____

Read Hebrews 11:5–6 and Genesis 5:18–24. For what did God reward Enoch?

_____

_____

_____

Faith in Hebrews 11:5–6 is directly connected to our actions. It is about looking to God as the ultimate source for our power. It is partially (but not entirely) about having hope in what we cannot see—Christ and the eternal life He offers in an eternal place. Enoch's actions, and the actions of all the people described in Hebrews 11, involve obediently following God's will. These actions stem from faith in Him. Faith in God precedes everything good, because He is the source of faith. It is not our efforts that God's work depends upon; it is God in whom we place faith. In light of this, what pleases God—merely placing faith *in* Him, or acting out of His faith in us?

_____

_____

_____

Read Hebrews 11:7 and Genesis 6–9. How did Noah condemn the world? Isn't God the only one who can condemn the world? Was Noah a co-actor in this event or did his actions solidify the divine indictment against humanity?

_____

_____

_____

Of what did Noah become an heir? How do we become righteous? Does it involve faith in God?

_____

_____

_____

SEEING THINGS FOR WHAT THEY REALLY ARE

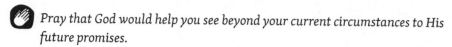

Pray that God would help you see beyond your current circumstances to His future promises.

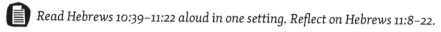

Read Hebrews 10:39–11:22 aloud in one setting. Reflect on Hebrews 11:8–22.

Underline all the verbs (action words) in the following verses:

> By faith Abraham obeyed when he was called to go out to a place that he was to receive as an inheritance. And he went out, not knowing where he was going. By faith he went to live in the land of promise, as in a foreign land, living in tents with Isaac and Jacob, heirs with him of the same promise. For he was looking forward to the city that has foundations, whose designer and builder is God. (Heb 11:8–10 ESV)

Read Genesis 17. The author of Hebrews sees a trajectory in this story. Abraham was promised the land, Moses led the people to it, and Joshua took it. David's son Solomon then built God's temple in the land. The holiness of the temple, as well as the city and land in which it was built, are symbolic of God's most holy place in heaven. Hebrews 9:1–10:18 expounds upon this. According to the author of Hebrews, Abraham's work was leading up to us entering God's most holy place.

Read Hebrews 11:11–12 and Genesis 18 and 21:1–7. Did Sarah have faith right away? What did God accomplish through Abraham and Sarah?

_____

_____

_____

_____

Read Hebrews 11:13–16. The faithful died believing, not trying to believe. Are we also "strangers and exiles on the earth"? What are we yet to receive? What homeland are we yet to visit?

_____

_____

_____

_____

_____

_____

_____

THE PERFECT USING THE IMPERFECT

Pray that God would show you how He can use even your imperfections for His perfect work.

Read Hebrews 10:39–11:22 aloud in one setting.

Read Genesis 22. Do you interpret Genesis 22 the same way as the author of Hebrews? In light of how the events in Genesis 22 end, what does the author of Hebrews mean when he says, "figuratively speaking, [Abraham] did receive [Isaac] back"?

_____

_____

_____

_____

_____

_____

Read Genesis 27. Why does the author of Hebrews speak so highly of people who made so many mistakes? Who is a more important character in these events—the human characters or the unseen God? If God can use these flawed people, what does that tell us about how He can use us?

_____

_____

_____

_____

Read Genesis 48–49, especially 49:28–33. Was Joseph's command to his descendants prophetic? (See Joshua 24:32.) Why did Joseph want his descendants to bring his bones to another land? Symbolically, what land are we waiting for (Heb 11:13–16)? How does this change your outlook on life?

_____

_____

_____

_____

_____

_____

WHAT MATTERS TO GOD

Pray that God would give you perspective—to understand what does and doesn't matter.

Read Hebrews 10:39–11:31 aloud in one setting. Reflect on Hebrews 11:8–22.

Underline all the verbs in verses 23–28.

Read Exodus 2 and 12. The author of Hebrews speaks of Moses considering "the reproach of Christ," but Moses encountered Yahweh in the wilderness (Exod 3), not Christ. What can we learn about the relationship between the God Moses encountered long before Christ was born, and Christ Himself, by the author's exchange of Yahweh (or LORD) for Christ?

_____

_____

_____

_____

_____

How did Moses endure (Heb 11:27)? What can we learn from Moses' perseverance?

_____

_____

_____

_____

_____

Read Exodus 14 and Joshua 6. What is the connection between the parting of the Red Sea and what happened at Jericho? What can we learn from these stories about how God acts?

_____

_____

_____

_____

_____

Reflect on Joshua 6:25. A "friendly welcome" is important to God because God cares for the outsider (Exod 23:12; Deut 1:16). What can you do to welcome outsiders into your community and home?

_____

_____

_____

_____

_____

GOD NEVER PROMISED US A HAPPY-GO-LUCKY LIFESTYLE

Pray that God would show you how He can use even your imperfections for His perfect work.

Read Hebrews 10:39–11:40 aloud in one setting.

Read Judges 6. What does Gideon do that was touched on in Hebrews 11:31?

_____

_____

_____

_____

Gideon, Barak (Judg 4–5), Samson (Judg 13–16), and Jephthah (Judg 11–12) were all judges who defended and resolved disputes for the tribes of Israel before they had a king. Samuel was the last judge who appointed Saul, and eventually David, as king (see 1 Samuel). Many people called by God have endured traumatic circumstances, but they have also witnessed God's amazing acts.

Some have seen the power of fire (1 Kgs 18:20–40), escaped death (1 Sam 19), have been made mighty in war and driven off foreign armies (Judg 7–8), and witnessed the resurrection of others (1 Kgs 17:17–24). Is it possible for us to see things as incredible as those God's people in the ancient world witnessed?

_____

_____

_____

_____

What did the people God called long ago not see (Heb 11:39–40)? Why did they not see it? What has God provided us with?

_____

_____

_____

_____

_____

_____

_____

WHEN IN DOUBT, LOOK TO THE FOUNDER

Pray that God would show you new ways to look at the founder of our faith.

Read Hebrews 10:39–12:2 aloud in one setting. Reflect on Hebrews 12:1–2.

Underline all the verbs Hebrews 12:1–2. Make a complete list of all the verbs used in the passages in the last few studies. When we have faith in God, it is by His power and out of His infinite wisdom that we can do what He has asked us. Everything is done through faith in Him.

_____

_____

_____

_____

_____

_____

Who is the cloud of witnesses, and what are they witnessing (Heb 12:1a)? What should we lay aside and why (Heb 12:1b–2)? If all else fails, on whom should we lean (12:2)?

_____

_____

_____

_____

_____

_____

_____

CONCLUSION

There are suggestions everywhere for where to place faith. But there are few suggestions that offer an eternal hope and a vast cloud of witnesses as testimony. Faith doesn't have to be abstract—it just has to be placed in the proper context. May you realize that the context is Christ. And may you find that faith in Christ is real and lasting.

HEBREWS 12

When we're frustrated with life, we often end up angry with God. We cry out, "Where are you? Why did you do this?" We become hostile toward God because we believe that His inability to act is the reason for our problems. Being angry is easier than dealing with the real issues: It's usually a case of simple cause and effect, or our own actions, which landed us in the tight spot.

The author of Hebrews holds back no punches about this in chapter 12. "You have *not* yet resisted *to the point* of shedding your blood as you struggle against sin. (12:4; italics added). This remark comes after we have been encouraged to "hold fast" to Christ (3:6; 4:14)—who Himself held fast to the point of suffering and execution. It also comes after a list of others who had faith *without* seeing God's promises fulfilled (11:13).

Warning: Blood, sweat, and tears are sometimes required. Nonetheless, there is surprising hope in the midst of suffering.

LAY ASIDE EVERY WEIGHT

Pray that the Holy Spirit would help you to place your worries and pain on Christ's shoulders.

Read Hebrews 11–12 aloud in one setting. Reflect on Hebrews 12:1–4.

Read Matthew 11:25–30. How can we "lay aside every weight and sin" (12:1)? Make a mental list of the weights and sins which are "clinging closely" in your life. Continue to ask God to take them from you each day.

_____

_____

_____

_____

How can we "run with endurance the race set before us" (12:1–2)? Hebrews 11 provides some examples.

_____

_____

_____

What should we keep in mind that Jesus did for us when faced with sin, opposition and burdens (12:3–4)? Our situations may be difficult, but with Christ we can overcome.

_____

_____

_____

_____

DISCIPLINE = LOVE?

Pray that the Holy Spirit would help you discern moments when God is teaching you discipline.

Read Hebrews 11:1–12:11 aloud in one setting. Reflect Hebrews 12:5–11.

Hebrews 12:5-6 contains a quotation from the Greek translation of Proverbs 3:11–12 (compare Psa 94:12). The Greek term translated "discipline" (paideuō, παιδεύω) in Hebrews 12:5–11 can also be translated "correction" or "instruction." We are enduring pain and suffering so that we can be instructed in God's school—be trained like an Olympic athlete. God takes tragic circumstances and does something great with them. God allows for cause and effect to guide much of our lives—He knows that we will learn through the process. Hebrews 12:9 is not a reference to God sending struggles and pain our way; instead, it indicates that following Christ will be inevitably marked by opposition because of our allegiance to Him.

In the moment, how does "correction" (discipline) feel? What does it produce (12:11)?

_____

_____

_____

_____

Do you agree with the author of Hebrews about discipline? Can you cite examples from your life where you have seen this principle at work?

_____

_____

_____

_____

LIFT YOUR HANDS, STRENGTHEN YOUR KNEES

Pray that Christ would give you strength to face challenges.

Read Hebrews 11:23–12:13 aloud in one setting. Reflect on Hebrews 12:12–13.

Hebrews 12:12 is not a pick-yourself-up-by-your-bootstraps message. In the context of the book, it is about taking the actions necessary to lean upon God so that you (and He) can have victory in your life. What is God calling you to do (Heb 12:12–13)?

_____

_____

_____

_____

_____

List all the areas of your life where God's strength needs to prevail. Write down specific examples. Ask someone you trust to put their hands on your shoulders and call out to God on your behalf. Don't be afraid to ask for help—we all need it.

_____

_____

_____

_____

_____

_____

_____

GOD THROUGH THE LENS OF PEACE AND HOLINESS

🤲 *Pray that God would teach you how to be peaceful and set apart (holy) for Him.*

📄 *Read Hebrews 11:39–12:17 aloud in one setting. Reflect on Hebrews 12:14–17.*

What should we strive for with everyone (12:14)? Why should we strive for it (12:14)?

_____

_____

_____

The author of Hebrews earnestly wants everyone to receive the grace of God, which is given directly by God. It results in us being free and redeemed. Grace is also given by us to others when they fall short (12:15). Why is it important that we emphasize these two elements in our communities?

_____

_____

_____

Hebrews 12:16–17 cites an example from Genesis 25–27—read this story. Like Esau, we have been given a gift: salvation. The author warns us not to sell this blessing for anything because we (like Esau) may not be given a chance to turn back to God again. We never know when our last day will come.

_____

_____

_____

TREMBLING IN FEAR IS NOT ALWAYS A BAD THING

Pray that God would teach you what a great privilege it is to approach Him.

Read Hebrews 12:1–21 aloud in one setting. Reflect on Hebrews 12:18–21.

The seven points the author lists in 12:18–19 describe the scene of the giving of the Law to the Israelites (Exod 19–20). Read Exodus 19–20. Should we fear God? Might it be said that there are two kinds of fear: Fear out of awe and respect; and fear from danger? Which kind occurs in Exodus 19–20? Which kind should we have?

_____

_____

_____

_____

Hebrews 12:19 is alluding to when, out of fear, the Israelites requested Moses speak to God instead of them (Exod 20:19). Likewise, Moses was afraid (Heb 12:22). By citing these examples, what is the author implying about our situation and the changes we need to make? List several examples and pray about them.

_____

_____

_____

_____

_____

_____

OFF TO SEE THE JUDGE OF ALL

🖐 *Pray that "the Mediator of the New Covenant" in heaven would also become your guide on earth.*

📄 *Read Hebrews 12:1–24 aloud in one setting. Reflect on Hebrews 12:22–24.*

What is the description in 12:22–24 contrasted against?

_____

_____

_____

_____

_____

_____

Search for two terms using Biblia.com or Bible software: (1) "Mount Zion" and (2) "heavenly Jerusalem." Where else are these terms used? In what context are they used? What light do the other biblical occurrences of these terms shed on Hebrews 12:22–24?

_____

_____

_____

_____

_____

_____

_____

Read Hebrews 1. What parallels are there in Hebrews 1 and Hebrews 12:22–24? In both scenes, we are witnessing actions that occur in God's council, which is made up of other divine beings, like angels. What members of God's council are mentioned in 12:22–24? Who is the last member mentioned? How is He described?

_____

_____

_____

_____

_____

Look up Abel in the concordance in the back of your Bible or on Biblia.com. What is significant about "the blood of Abel"? How does Jesus' blood "speak a better word"? What is the effect of this "better word" on our lives?

_____

_____

_____

_____

_____

A VOICE THAT SHAKES THE EARTH

Pray that God's voice would be heard in every part of your life.

Read Hebrews 12:1–27 aloud in one setting. Reflect on Hebrews 12:25–27.

Hebrews 12:25 opens with a reference back to the giving of the Ten Commandments discussed in 12:22–24. Do you accept (and do) what God asks of you? Where do you fall short? If much of Hebrews is about suffering, what does this statement mean (12:25)?

_____

_____

_____

_____

_____

What will God do once more (12:26)? What implications does this have upon how we live here and now? If Christ was coming tomorrow to "shake the earth," what would you change about the way you are living right now?

_____

_____

_____

_____

_____

_____

A KINGDOM THAT CANNOT BE SHAKEN AND A CONSUMING FIRE

Pray that God would show you every day how you can serve His kingdom

Read Hebrews 12:1–29 aloud in one setting. Reflect on Hebrews 12:28–29.

For what should we be grateful (12:28)? What does God desire from us (12:28)?

_____

_____

_____

_____

_____

What conclusion can you draw about the phrase "our God is a consuming fire" (12:29)? Does it evoke ideas of fear or hope, or both? With this knowledge in mind, how should you approach God? How does this motif tie into the ideas about God's instruction and our relationship with other people in the community of God?

_____

_____

_____

_____

_____

_____

CONCLUSION

God is to be loved and feared. He is to be approached with awe and adoration. Our relationship with a God who is opposed to destruction, chaos and sin will always involve us opposing the same things. In doing so, we will be met by people and the powers of darkness with hostility. We will be tempted and struggle. However, we can have hope because God teaches us by using (not causing) these terrible things. This will enhance our eternal relationship with Him; and it doesn't get better than that. May you place your burdens on Christ. May you see God work through tragedies and turmoil in your life—bringing you ever closer to Him along the way.

HEBREWS 13

We all like a message of hope and grace, but when offering it to others our commitment is usually fleeting. This is obvious when great tragedy hits. There is an outpouring of compassion and aid for a few days, weeks, or months, but then the people who are still hurting are forgotten.

The author of Hebrews calls us to do more: Much of Christianity is about living graciously and being hopeful every day. After explaining the history of God's redemptive plan leading up to Christ, the author of Hebrews concludes with some commands and a little more theology. Not exactly what we all want to hear, but it's what we need to hear. In the next few studies, we will explore what it means to love one another as Christ loves us.

ENTERTAINING ANGELS

Pray that God would show you more ways that you can be hospitable and help the hurting.

Read Hebrews 13:1–25 aloud in one sitting. Reflect on Hebrews 13:1–3.

When interpreting the Bible, it's easy to displace its ancient context with our modern feelings. There are several examples of "brotherly love" that I would not want to represent. You know, the Cain and Abel type (Gen 4). We can't let our feelings about our brothers, or relationships, interfere with what God is trying to tell us. The "brotherly love" (*philadelphía, φιλαδελφία*) in Hebrews 13:1 is about sharing a common spiritual life (Rom 12:10; 1 Thess 4:9; 1 Pet 1:22; 2 Pet 1:7)—bearing each other's burdens as Christ bore ours. How can you better bear the burdens of your fellow believers?

_____

_____

_____

_____

_____

When was the last time you showed hospitality to a stranger? If you have to think about the answer, then you need to make a change. How can you find more opportunities to be hospitable to strangers? Christ didn't wait for opportunities to arise; He went to people (John 4).

_____

_____

_____

_____

Read Genesis 18:1–19:29. What light does this passage shed on what it means to "entertain angels without knowing it" (Heb 13:2)?

_____

_____

_____

_____

_____

In what way does God ask us to "remember the prisoners" (13:3)? How does this represent "brotherly love"? How can you bear the burdens of those in prison?

_____

_____

_____

_____

_____

Hebrews 13:3 is likely referring to Christians who are in prison because of their belief in Christ. Nonetheless, shouldn't we extend "brotherly love" to all who are hurting or imprisoned? Christ's love knew no bounds, and neither should ours. How can you show His love in your life? Think beyond just how you can show love in your current contexts to how you can find more opportunities to demonstrate it.

_____

_____

_____

_____

_____

NEVER LEFT OR FORSAKEN

Pray that the Holy Spirit would work in you to make you content.

Read Hebrews 13:1–16 aloud. Reflect on Hebrews 13:4–6.

Why do you think that marriage is emphasized next to verses about helping the hurting? What are we asked to do in our marriages (Heb 13:4)? Even if you are not married, how can you live by this commandment and help others to do so?

_____

_____

_____

Why must we keep our lives free from the "love of money" (13:5)? What can a "love of money" do to us? How does Hebrews 13:5 instruct us to break free from the hold finances have on our lives?

_____

_____

_____

_____

What can we confidently say when we are content (13:6)? Hebrews 13:6 is a paraphrase of Psalm 118:6, combined with a line from Psalm 56:4 (or 56:11). How can you live what Hebrews 13:6 teaches?

_____

_____

_____

_____

ALWAYS CONSIDER THE OUTCOME

Pray that Christ will show you the right teachers to follow.

Read Hebrews 13:1–16 aloud. Reflect on Hebrews 13:7–9.

What is the "outcome" of a Christ-centered leader's way of life (Heb 13:7)? Why should we imitate our Christ-focused leaders?

_____

_____

_____

_____

_____

_____

Does Jesus Christ change (13:8)? The natural conclusion of Christ not changing, but remaining the same, is that "strange teachings" are just that—new, strange, and not true (13:9). If they were truly of Christ, they would not be absurd or odd. They would align with what is professed in the New Testament through Christ's apostles and those who recorded His story.

_____

_____

_____

_____

_____

The "foods" referred to in 13:9 are the sacrifices that were being offered by the Jewish priesthood in the first century AD (13:10-11), and likely those being offered by Greek religious groups. However, it is not by the sacrifice of food that we are strengthened, but by Christ's grace.

The author's logic here is quite simple: Look at the outcome of what someone is doing. If the religious people are not getting closer to God, what does that tell you? Grace overcomes (13:9). Sacrifices and religion enslave. How can you break out of the mold of religiosity in your life and seek Christ's grace?

_____

_____

_____

_____

_____

AS JESUS SUFFERED, SO SHALL WE

Pray that God would strengthen you for when you have to bear reproach.

Read Hebrews 13:1–16 aloud. Reflect on Hebrews 13:10–14.

Hebrews 13:9 tells us to not be led away by the food (or sacrifices) of other religions. By comparison, think of the modern religions (Christian and non-Christian) that offer legalism instead of grace. The author of Hebrews goes on to directly condemn the Jewish leaders of his day (13:10). Why do the Jewish leaders—still serving the old religion based in legalism, instead of Christ who perfected grace—have no right to be at the altar Christ was offered upon (13:10; compare 1 Cor 10:14–22; Isa 53:10)?

_____

_____

_____

_____

_____

_____

The high priest (of the "old religion" and "Old Covenant") would regularly offer sacrifices. Where were they eventually burned (Heb 13:11; compare Lev 4:12, 21)? Jesus was crucified at Golgotha, which is outside the city of Jerusalem, similar to how the sacrifices that were made in the tabernacle (when the Hebrews lived in the desert) were taken outside the camp (Heb 13:11–12). Just as the sacrifices made in the tabernacle sanctified (purified the people before God), Jesus' blood spilt at Golgotha purified all of us (13:13).

To whom are we called to go, and who is our model for suffering when we are persecuted for our beliefs (13:13)? Why should we do this (13:14)? What lasting thing are we seeking (13:14)?

_____

_____

_____

_____

_____

_____

MODERN SACRIFICES

🤚 *Pray that God would help you identify what He desires for you to sacrifice.*

📄 *Read Hebrews 13:1–16 aloud. Reflect on Hebrews 13:15–17.*

What are we asked to do "through" Christ (Heb 13:15)? Why should we do this?

_____

_____

_____

_____

_____

What type of sacrifice does God require (13:15; compare Mic 6:6–8)?

_____

_____

_____

_____

_____

What should we never neglect (Heb 13:16)?

_____

_____

_____

_____

Adversity can be overcome with thanksgiving (Eph 5:15–21; Col 3:12–17). There is always something to be thankful for, even when it feels like there is not. The author of Hebrews was likely enduring pain for Christ (Heb 13:18–19), and we know for certain that the audience of the book was (10:32–34). But, for the author, that was no excuse to back down from what Christ had asked. Our eternal gift, salvation through Christ, can never be taken away from us. Why then are Christians so afraid? How can you stare down fear in your life and better embrace Christ's calling?

KEEPING WATCH OVER SOULS

Pray that the Holy Spirit would show you ways you can better serve your leaders.

Read Hebrews 13:17–21 aloud. Reflect on Hebrews 13:17.

In many churches I have attended or joined, there hasn't been enough respect for pastors, elders, and deacons. In most circumstances, our misgivings about these people seem justified. But even when they are justified, respect can go a long way. Whether these individuals were appointed by God, or they ended up in authority through cause and effect, the church will be better off if we love, help, and support them.

As long as a leader is not steering people away from Christ or being abusive, we should do what Hebrews 13:17 recommends. But why should we do so? Who holds our leaders accountable (13:17)?

_____

_____

_____

_____

_____

What are the leaders required to do (13:17)? How can you better support the leaders in your community? How can you show them "brotherly love" (13:1)?

_____

_____

_____

_____

_____

PRAY EARNESTLY

Pray that Christ would reveal to you who you should pray for regularly.

Read Hebrews 13:17–21 aloud. Reflect on Hebrews 13:18–19.

For what type of prayer does the author of Hebrews ask (13:18)? Why does the author ask for prayer (13:19)?

_____

_____

_____

_____

Who do you know that needs prayer? Take the rest of the time you would usually devote to studying Hebrews and reflect upon how you can pray for leaders in your church, community, nation, and world. Then, pray. When praying, be sure to take time to be silent and listen; prayer is a conversation.

_____

_____

_____

_____

_____

EQUIPPED BY THE BLOOD OF THE ETERNAL COVENANT

Pray that God would help you, via His Holy Spirit, to do His will.

Read Hebrews 13:1–25 aloud in one sitting. Reflect on Hebrews 13:20–25.

Read 1 Peter 1:1–4. What does it mean for us to have a "God of peace" (Heb 13:20)?

_____

_____

_____

_____

Read John 17. How is Christ's resurrection tied to God's ability to give us peace?

_____

_____

_____

_____

Read John 10:1–18. Compare Ezekiel 34:1–10. What does it mean for Christ to be our great shepherd (Heb 13:20–21)?

_____

_____

_____

_____

What does it mean that Christ gave us His blood as an eternal covenant
(contract) between us and God (Heb 13:21)? (Read Hebrews 8.)

_____

_____

_____

_____

What will Christ continue to do for us (Heb 13:20)? No matter what trials come
our way, no matter what pain we endure, we can be sure that Christ is with us
via His Holy Spirit and our brothers and sisters in Christ.

_____

_____

_____

_____

To whom does "glory" belong? How long will "glory" last (13:21)?

_____

_____

_____

_____

The book of Hebrews has two endings: One that ends with an "Amen" (13:21)
and one after the epilogue (13:22–25). This suggests that everything leading
up to 13:21 is a sermon. The author confirms this by calling Hebrews 1:1–13:21a
"word of exhortation"—the first century AD phrase for a sermon (13:22).
Hebrews is meant to be preached. So let's preach it by living it. May grace be
with you in doing so (13:25).

CONCLUSION

After working through Hebrews for this Bible study, I have a long mental list of ways this book is connected to everything we do. I now hear the words of this book in my head during my daily interactions with other people. But instead of offering my list, or my own hopes and prayers for you, I offer the author of Hebrews' closing words:

"Now may the God of peace who brought again from the dead our Lord Jesus, the great shepherd of the sheep, by the blood of the eternal covenant, equip you with everything good that you may do his will, working in us that which is pleasing in his sight, through Jesus Christ, to whom be glory forever and ever. Amen.... Grace be with all of you."

Make Your Bible Study Even Better

Get 30% off Bible Study Magazine.